Swivel-Head

Susan Gates

Illustrated by Martin Remphry

OXFORD
UNIVERSITY PRESS

D1396410

For Christopher

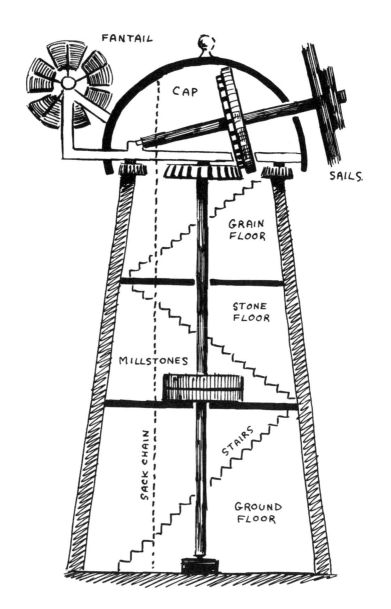

FANTAIL

CAP

SAILS.

GRAIN FLOOR

STONE FLOOR

MILLSTONES

SACK CHAIN

STAIRS

GROUND FLOOR

CHAPTER 1

Mr Popular

My mum's inherited a windmill.

That's right – a windmill.

Mum inherited it from her cousin. It's called Blezzard's Mill and it's two hundred years old.

And we've just moved here, Mum, Dad and me, to live in it.

I've got to make new friends, start a new school, everything. I'm standing in front of my new school now. It's my first day and Mum's just dropped me off in Flying Bull Lane. The school's called, you've guessed it, Flying Bull Lane School. I could be thinking, 'That's a stupid name.' But my head's full of much more serious thoughts. Such as: 'I wish I wasn't here. I wish I was back where we used to live.'

Mum's just about to drive away and leave me. But, before she does, she winds down the car window to have a few last words. She doesn't feel a stranger here like I do. She was born in this village. 'I used to go to this school,' she tells me. 'It's a lovely school. You'll like it.'

But I'm thinking about my old school – the one I used to go to. It had a *sensible* name: Park View Junior School. I would have been in Mrs Miller's class this year. I liked her – she was a really good teacher.

Mum seems to read my mind. She frowns and looks upset. 'You'll soon get used to it here,' she says. 'You'll soon make some new friends.'

I don't like my mum getting upset. So I slap a big, cheesy grin on my face and pretend I'm super-confident. ''Course I'll make friends,' I tell her. 'No problemo. Don't worry about me. I'm Mr Popular, I am.' I thump my chest like Tarzan. 'I'll have loads of friends by home time, you'll see. Bet I bring someone back for tea.'

Mum grins and says, 'Give me six.'

We slap hands together. Then she drives away, past a pub called The Miller's Thumbs – this place is full of the weirdest names.

I look up to where Mum's going – to Blezzard's Mill, our new home. It's on top of a hill. You can see it for miles around. It's a great, black tower like a lighthouse, with a dome on top like a giant white onion – that's called the cap. And it's got four massive white sails in a cross shape. They don't go round though. The windmill was working right up until last year. But now there's no one to run it. Not since Mum's cousin died.

We don't live *inside* the windmill. We're living in the mill house next door. The windmill's still full of ancient machinery for grinding corn into flour – mill stones and creaky wooden gear-wheels and all sorts of dusty old junk. My dad will soon clear that out though. He's got big plans for Blezzard's Mill.

Drrrringgg. There goes the school bell. I tear my eyes away from our windmill and walk into Flying Bull Lane School. I've got my right hand hidden inside my cuff. I almost forgot to mention – it was Mum saying, 'Give me six,' that reminded me – I've got six fingers on my right hand. Four fingers and two thumbs, actually.

It doesn't bother me, so you needn't feel sorry for me or be embarrassed to talk about it or anything. I could have had an operation to cut off my spare thumb. But I like it. It gets me friends quicker than anything. It makes me the centre of attention. I say, 'Give me six,' and, at first, kids look at me as if I'm completely dumb. They shake their heads and say, 'You mean give me *five*, don't you?'

Then, like a magician pulling flowers from up

his sleeve, I pull out my right hand, waggle my fingers and say, 'Count 'em.' And they say, 'One, two, three, four, five, *six?*'

Then their eyes usually pop out and they say things like, 'That's weird. You an alien or something?' And I usually reply, in a really cool way, 'I was born like it.'

And they usually say, 'Wow,' again. They're pretty impressed. They think having an extra thumb is something special. Freaky – but special.

I expect the kids at Flying Bull Lane will think it's special too. But I don't need to waggle my six digits at them straight away. I'll keep them in reserve until I need them. They're my secret weapon for making friends.

In the classroom a boy says, 'What's your name, new kid?'

'Simon Trill,' I tell him, keeping my thumbs out of sight in my pocket.

He looks like my kind of friend. He looks like Mr Cool, the coolest kid in Flying Bull Lane School. He's got really great clothes and trainers with silver streaks that must have cost about a hundred pounds.

10

'Where do you live?' he asks me.

I jerk my head towards the window. You can see Blezzard's Mill from the classroom. I give it a quick glance. Then something, I don't know what, makes me take a longer look. Our windmill looks strange. Quite sinister really. Like a giant black robot marching over the hill top.

'What? You're the new people from Blezzard's Mill?' asks the cool kid.

'Yeah,' I shrug. 'You can come back after school, if you want to.' I try to make my invitation sound casual, as if it doesn't matter to me whether he comes or not.

But I can't help adding, 'We can play computer games.'

Not in my bedroom though. He might see the bell on the wall. There's this big, rusty old bell, right? And it used to be connected by wires to the windmill. It's an alarm bell or something, to wake the miller up if he's having a nap. To let him know that something's gone wrong in the mill. I told Mum, 'Take that mouldy old bell away. It ruins my bedroom.' But you know what she said? She said, 'We can't do that. That bell's an antique. And anyway, it's part of the mill's character.' How can a mill have a *character*? I ask you.

Mr Cool isn't thrilled by my invitation. 'I've got some really great computer games,' I tell him, just to encourage him.

What he does next really shakes me. He makes a pop-eyed face. (And I haven't even shown him my extra thumb yet.) He waves his hands like he's driving wasps away. Then he yells, 'No way, I'm not coming up there! Everyone knows there's a ghost in that windmill. It's *haunted*,' he tells me in a low, spooky voice. 'Everyone says so. You must be crazy to live up there.'

Things aren't going too well. So I tell myself, 'Simon, time for your secret weapon.'

I whip my right hand out my pocket and say, 'Give me six.'

Then I wait for Mr Cool's mouth to make a big, round 'Wow!' It's infallible. But,

I can't believe it, all he does is *shrug*. He doesn't look surprised at all. He even yawns, as if he's bored or something.

This isn't what should happen. What's going on? For a second, I feel all hot and confused and panicky, as if the world is playing tricks on me.

Then I start making excuses for him: 'Maybe he needs glasses. Maybe he's brainless – maybe he doesn't know how many fingers and thumbs people are *supposed* to have.'

So I count them for him, very slowly to make sure he understands. 'Look – one, two, three, four, five, *six*. I've got one more than you have.'

'So?' he says, shrugging again. He understands all right. He's just not impressed. Not even slightly curious.

Then he says something even stranger. 'You're one of *them*, aren't you? You're a Blezzard.'

'Naa, I'm not.'

'Come on,' he says, in an accusing voice. 'You must be.'

'Well, my mum's name was Blezzard. But she married my dad and now she's a Trill.'

'Aha,' he says, narrowing his eyes, as if I've confessed to a really bad habit. 'I knew you were related to them.'

Then he says to a girl sitting on her own in the corner, 'Hey, he's one of your lot. He can sit next to you.'

And he shoves me towards her and turns away. As if he's not interested in me any more!

I'm not used to being treated this way – I'm getting more and more confused. Without even thinking, I lift my hand up to the girl and say, 'Give me six.'

And she does.

It's my turn to go goggle-eyed. What kind of weird school is this? This girl has got *two* thumbs on her right hand – just like me.

'Hello,' she says. 'I'm Prudence Blezzard.'

'Errrrr. Hi.'

I can't stop gawping. I don't mean to be rude

and it's not as if I've never seen a two-thumbed hand. I mean, I see one every day, don't I? It's just that I've never seen one on *another person*.

Her spare thumb isn't the only freaky thing about her. She's a sort of giant girl. I feel like a weedy shrimp beside her. She's tall and strong with red rosy cheeks and a big moon-face and brown plaits with red and yellow elastic bands wound round the ends of them.

She's got black wellies on. They're splattered with what looks like green mud. I don't want to look too hard, or smell too hard either. Because I don't think it's mud. I think it's cow plop. And she's wearing a woolly hat the colour of cow plop too. (Only it looks like a tea cosy.) And layers of woolly jumpers and cardigans. She's wrapped up like a pass-the-parcel. Her jumpers look like Granny knitted them. Or like they came from a jumble sale.

I think you've guessed it by now. Prudence Blezzard, the girl *I'm* sitting next to, is the uncoolest kid in Flying Bull Lane School. Probably in the world or even the universe.

'This is a bad start, Simon,' I tell myself. 'A really bad start.'

'Phew, this classroom is stuffy,' she says.

Then she bounces up out of her seat and starts peeling off woolly jumpers! I don't know where to look – a blue one, an orange one, a purple one. Like she's taking off a rainbow. But she's still got plenty of them left underneath.

My eyes are wide open. My mouth is too. She plonks herself down again and sees me staring at her.

'It's freezing cold up where I live,' she explains. 'You have to dress warm. Or you get frost bite and chilblains.'

'Where – where do you live?' I stutter.

'Up there,' she says, pointing up the hill to Blezzard's Mill.

'But I live there,' I say, stupidly.

'No, not the *windmill*, silly. We live in the farm next to it. High Cold Knott Farm, that's where *we* live.'

I look to where she's pointing. About two fields away from the windmill there's a tumble-down stone cottage with some tumble-down barns and buildings round it.

'What a dump,' I'm thinking to myself. 'I'd be ashamed to tell anyone I lived there. I'd keep it a secret.'

But she's not bothered at all. Not about where she lives or the cow plop on her wellies, or her jumble-sale jumpers or her tea-cosy hat or being called *Prudence*. Any other kid would have the decency to be embarrassed.

I wouldn't be seen dead sitting next to her. Not normally. But I've got no choice, have I? Because no one else has asked me. They seem to think that Prudence and I *belong* together. Are they trying to insult me or something?

But things get worse. Prudence is busy sharpening a pencil. She twists it round and round in the sharpener until it's almost sharpened to nothing. Then she suddenly booms at me, in a really loud voice, 'Is your mum called Prudence?'

I cringe and look round to see if anyone heard. 'No she *isn't*,' I hiss back at her.

She doesn't look surprised. 'Well,' she says, 'not all of us Blezzards are called Prudence. None of the boys is, of course, ha, ha! They're called

Noah, mostly. My dad's called Noah. And my brother is.'

'Well, I'm not called Noah, am I? I'm not even called Blezzard. I'm a Trill.'

'But your mum's a Blezzard,' Prudence points out, in a matter-of-fact way. 'So we must be related, mustn't we?'

'No, we're *not*,' I say, getting really flustered. 'My mum only lived here until she was six.'

'Doesn't matter,' Prudence says, calmly. 'We're still related. Once a Blezzard always a Blezzard, that's what my dad says.'

By now, I'm squirming inside. I don't want to be a Blezzard. No way!

'We must be related somehow,' she says. 'Because you've got miller's thumbs.'

'What? Miller's thumbs? What are you talking about?' I yell, right into her face.

I think I'm getting a bit hysterical. I might *even* be losing my cool.

Prudence just flicks her plaits out the way and says, 'Shh. Stop shouting. Here's Miss.'

Miss *seems* like a perfectly *normal* teacher. Phew, that's a big relief.

She says, 'Hello Simon.' And I mumble, 'Hello.' She says, 'Welcome to Flying Bull Lane School,' and I just wag my head like a nodding dog. She must think I'm stupid but I can't help that. I'm all mixed up – I've had too many nasty shocks. My brain feels like our washing machine. It's whirling round and round and round with Blezzards and haunted windmills and miller's thumbs all tangled together inside it.

CHAPTER 2

Us Blezzards

It's over at last. My first, disastrous day at Flying Bull Lane School. And I'm walking back home through the village with Prudence Blezzard.

I know. *I know* I said I wouldn't be seen dead with her. But I've got to invite *someone* home, haven't I? My mum will be expecting it. She's probably made some cakes specially.

Prudence is striding along in her big, clumpy wellies. They make her walk like a man on the moon.

We go clumping past the church. You can't see the big window from here, it's round the back. Mum says there's a picture of our mill in that window, made out of stained glass. It looks just like it did two hundred years ago. There's even a tiny miller climbing out along the sails. I must go and look at it some time.

'Look, *there* are the miller's thumbs,' booms Prudence, right out of the blue.

'Where? Where?' I say, startled, whipping my head round.

'No, up there.' She's pointing above our heads.

There's the pub sign swinging just above us. It's weird. It's got a massive hand on it, big as a shovel. And the hand is holding up two monster thumbs.

'Like our hands,' says Prudence.

I'm not stupid, I can see that. I grunt some kind of reply. *'Nerrr.'*

I don't want to encourage her. She's only a temporary friend. I'll make a *proper* friend tomorrow. How was I to know my thumbs wouldn't work this time? They've never let me down before.

'Lots of us Blezzards have got spare thumbs,' Prudence is telling me. 'My mum says it runs in the family.'

I can't help wincing, as if I've got toothache. This is so embarrassing. I wish she wouldn't speak so loud, as if she's shouting across three fields. I wish she wouldn't keep saying, 'us Blezzards' as if she's including me.

'And those of us who were millers were dead famous for having an extra thumb,' she says as she stomps along beside me. 'I'll tell you about it, if you like.'

'Don't bother,' I mutter. But she goes ahead anyway.

'See, all millers have got one miller's thumb. That's the thumb they use to rub the flour with, to test if it's grinding fine enough. It's their right hand thumb, usually. But us Blezzards, we just happen to have two miller's thumbs on our right hands. Twice the rubbing power! So that's lucky isn't it? If you're a miller, that is –'

'Oh yeah, really lucky,' I tell her, raising my eyebrows. She doesn't seem to notice I'm being sarcastic.

'Look.' She rubs her two thumbs against her fingers. It makes a dry, rustly noise, like grasshoppers' legs. 'That's what millers do all the time, testing the flour. You try it.'

'No thanks,' I say, frowning and shaking my head.

I've got my right hand stuffed in my pocket and I'm going to keep it there. But I can still feel my two thumbs. I'm starting to hate those miller's thumbs. Round here, *everyone* knows what they mean. They mean I'm one of them – a Blezzard – 'Wait a minute, why hasn't my mum got miller's thumbs?' I ask Prudence excitedly. 'If she's a *Blezzard*, why hasn't she got 'em?'

There's a flash of wild hope in my brain.

Maybe Mum isn't a Blezzard at all! Maybe she was adopted or found abandoned on a doorstep or something.

'Not all of us have 'em,' says Prudence.

'Oh.'

She isn't surprised about my mum. Nothing much seems to surprise her.

'My grandad didn't have miller's thumbs,' she explains in her slow-talking way. 'But Dad does and my brother Noah does. Some of us do. Some of us don't. Your mum must be one of the ones that don't.'

'Oh, right.' My hopes have come crashing down again.

And I've just noticed it's been growing dark. As if it's night-time instead of afternoon. There's a cold, gusty wind blowing down the street. The Miller's Thumbs sign swings, *creak, creak,* over our heads.

Prudence checks the sky as if she's an expert on the weather.

'There's a storm coming,' she says. 'We'd better run home, quick.'

I look up at Blezzard's Mill. Thunder clouds

are gathering round it. The sails have gone dark, like a giant, black cross on the hill top. For a minute our mill looks sinister, threatening – just like it did this morning. And that makes me remember something.

'That kid this morning – the cool kid with the silver trainers. He said our windmill was haunted. He said there was a ghost in it. He was just winding me up, wasn't he? Just having a joke, ha, ha? I mean, I didn't take him *seriously*, of course.'

It takes Prudence even longer than usual to reply. When she does I wish she hadn't bothered.

'Some kids round here do think it's haunted. They won't go up there. They won't go anywhere near it. They say there are noises at night. And some of them say they've seen things.'

'What things?' My voice isn't sarcastic now. It's shaky and scared. I've started trembling – I can't help it. It feels like icy thumbs are pressing into my spine.

But Prudence just shrugs. She doesn't seem very worried. 'Oh – things,' she says. 'But I don't believe it. It's just kids making up spooky stories. And Noah doesn't believe it either. He knows every corner of your windmill 'cos he used to work there.'

She goes clumping away.

'Which Noah are you talking about?' I yell after her.

'OUR NOAH,' she roars back.

Suddenly, the rain comes sizzling down.

Where's she gone? I can't see her. Everything's blurry grey. The rain's pinging like dried peas off the top of my head.

I could put my hood up, but I won't. No way. It's a bright yellow one with a beaky bit at the front – it makes me look like a chicken.

So I just scrunch my head down into my shoulders and go staggering up the hill.

The rain's hissing like Medusa's snaky hair. The wind's pushing me one way, pulling me another. Now it's thumping me, *biff, biff,* as if I'm a punch bag.

'In here!' a voice bellows. And a six-fingered hand shoots out, grabs my coat and yanks me inside.

I collapse inside a door and gasp, 'Phew, where'd that rain come from? It's mega-stormy out there.'

'It's only a shower,' says Prudence, calmly. 'The sun'll come out in a minute.'

It's gone very quiet. I can hardly hear the wind. I blink the rain out of my eyes and start sneezing, *'Achoo! Achoo!'* I'm sprawled on some dusty old sacks of grain. And I've just realized where we are.

We're inside Blezzard's Mill.

CHAPTER 3

Inside the mill

I stagger to my feet. *'Aaaaargh,'* and go crashing down in a cloud of white dust. My shoes are tangled in something. There's a shining chain hooked round my ankles. In a panic, I try to kick myself free.

'It's only the sack hoist,' says Prudence. 'Just keep still.'

She crouches down to unhook the chain. 'It's what the miller uses to pull the sacks to the top of the mill. Look, that's where it goes.'

She points to a trapdoor. It's right above our heads. It's closed but there's a hole in it where the chain slides through.

'See, this chain goes all the way to the top of the mill. The miller gives a couple of tugs on the chain. And someone down here hooks on a sack and it gets pulled to the top floor. Then the miller tips the corn out and it drops through a chute-thing into the mill stones and comes down here again through some more chutes. Only, hey presto, it's flour now, not corn.'

'I know how a windmill works.'

I do know, actually. I'm not just trying to be clever. My dad doesn't know anything about windmills – he's an accountant. But my mum knows a bit.

She used to come to this mill when she was a little girl.

The first time we looked round our mill she told me how all the machinery worked. How the sails turned the big wooden gear-wheels and they turned the stones and that ground the corn.

When she told me all this I said, 'Yeah, Mum, yeah,' in my bored-to-death voice. She could see that I wasn't interested, so she didn't explain any more. She kept it to herself.

Prudence seems even keener than Mum about windmills. Maybe it's a Blezzard thing. Something only Blezzards understand. Maybe they're windmill freaks. Well, I'm not like them. I'm a Trill. To tell the truth, I don't like windmills at all. That proves I'm not like them, doesn't it?

Prudence is heading for the wooden steps that lead up to the next floor.

'I'm going up to the stone floor,' she says.

Suppose I'd better go with her. I give a big sigh, grab hold of the sack hoist chain and haul myself to my feet.

I'm standing under the trapdoor, still holding the chain, when I feel two tugs.

'Naa,' I tell myself. 'You imagined it.'

But there's no mistake. *Tug, tug* – there it goes again. Someone up there is pulling on the sack hoist chain. Just as if the miller was sending down a message, 'Hook on another sack.'

I let the chain go as if it's red-hot. It must have been Prudence.

It's not Prudence. I can still see her. Her wellies are only just disappearing off the top step. So who else is up there? I try peering through the hole in the trapdoor, where the chain glides through. But I can't see a thing, only the silver chain, snaking up into the dark.

Suddenly, I feel scared down here on my own. So I go scrambling up the steps after Prudence, to the stone floor where the millstones are.

This floor's crammed with old wooden machinery. I don't know what any of it is.

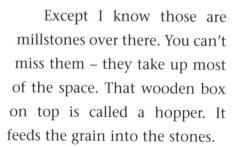

Except I know those are millstones over there. You can't miss them – they take up most of the space. That wooden box on top is called a hopper. It feeds the grain into the stones.

Wait a second, how do I know that? How do I know it's called a

34

hopper? No one told me that; I'm sure they didn't – but they must have done. Someone must have told me. Else how do I *know*?

I don't want to think about it. I look out the window instead. There's a sail! So close, that if I opened the window and stretched out my hand, I could nearly touch it –

'Simon?'

'Prudence, where are you?'

'I'm up here. On the bin floor.'

I go clattering up more creaky steps and, *pow*, it's dark again. The windows are shuttered up here. I can just make out the bins where they store the grain. There's not much else to see. There's no one here but us. I even check in the big wooden bins. They're empty. I can feel the hair prickling on the back of my neck.

'That sack hoist –' I try to tell her.

'Yep, it comes all the way up here,' says Prudence, pointing to the floor, where the chain comes up through a hole in another trapdoor.

I follow it up and up, with my mouth hanging open.

'Where's it go? Aren't we at the top of the mill

yet?'

'No, it's got one more floor yet, the cap floor. And then we're right at the very top.'

We go up again. Whoever tugged on that chain *must* be up there. There's nowhere else for him to be.

When we get to the top floor I can't see much at first. It's dark, full of secrets. I can feel wind on my face. Where's that coming from? It seems to be coming through the walls.

'Prudence?'

The sack chain rattles as I blunder about.

'Where are you?'

Then suddenly, there's dazzling light everywhere. Glittery white dust is blowing all round me. I look upwards.

'Wow!'

I can see straight up into the white dome. It's like the brain-box of the mill up there. A clockwork brain-box, cramful of wheels and shafts and gears. All sorts of crazy, old-fashioned machinery.

And Prudence is up there. Right inside the machinery, on top of a little ladder. She's opened

a hatch and she's gazing out at the sky. It looks as if she could walk out onto the clouds.

When she sees me, she comes clumping back down the ladder.

'That's the brake wheel,' she says, pointing to a massive wheel in the cap. 'If that brake wasn't on, the sails would be turning. Then all this machinery would be working –' She looks dreamy, as if she can see it coming to life inside her head.

I'm looking around. There's no one else up here. It's not scary. It's light and breezy and silvery with drifting dust.

Then all of a sudden, Prudence says, 'Have you seen him?'

That scares me to death.

'Who? Who?' I spin round like a dancer doing a twirl. 'Who's there?'

'No, silly, I mean *him*.'

When I see where she's pointing, I feel really stupid. It's just a name, carved onto a beam. It's hard to make it out. I read it out loud.

NOAH BLEZZARD 1805

'Noah Blezzard, 1805. Who's he?' I'm pleased by how steady my voice sounds – it's hardly shaking at all.

'He's the first of us Blezzards that worked this mill, of course.' Prudence says it as if it's something the whole world knows about but me. 'The first miller always carves his name in the mill.'

'How come you know so much about windmills?' I interrupt her.

The answer she gives is exactly the one I don't want to hear.

She shrugs and says, 'All us Blezzards know about windmills. We were *born* knowing about windmills. We've got windmills in our blood.'

I don't want to hear any more. I want to block up my ears and run far away. But she says, 'You're quite weird for a Blezzard, you know. Because you don't know much about windmills and you're not called Noah –'

I want to yell out a protest, '*I'm* not weird. *I'm* a perfectly normal kid. It's *you* lot that are weird. Normal kids don't know about windmills!'

But, somehow, I can't yell out. It's this place – it's the kind of place where you speak in whispers, as if you're in a cathedral. So I just sigh and mutter, 'For heaven's sake.'

Then I think, 'If she knows so much about windmills, then she can tell me why I felt those pulls on that sack hoist chain, when there's nobody up here to pull it.'

I really want to know because it spooks you, something like that. But I daren't ask her. I don't want to look like a fool. And anyhow I'm already beginning to think, 'Perhaps I only imagined it.'

'Have you seen the view?' asks Prudence. 'From up in the cap where I was just now? Come and look. You can see right to the coast.'

She goes clumping up the ladder, right into the dome, among the wheels and cogs and gears.

'Come on!' she bawls down at me. I wish she wouldn't shout like that.

The ladder's rickety. I have to duck out the way of all the giant clockwork machinery. Good job the sails aren't turning. If the sails were turning then these wheels would be turning and my head would get ripped off. This whole cap can turn! Did you know that? It can swivel like a head to bring the sails into the wind's eye –

Oh no. How do I know all that? Those facts slipped out – just ignore them. I don't know *anything* about windmills. Honest, I don't. Not that they've got swivelling heads. Not *anything*.

Suddenly I'm squeezed on the top rung of the ladder with Prudence and the wind is blasting into my face.

'Look at that.' I can't help being impressed. I can see for miles from up here, right over the countryside. I can see the mill house and High Cold Knott Farm, where Prudence lives.

The sheep in her fields look like white cotton wool blobs.

We can see right down to the village. I can see the church and The Miller's Thumbs pub and Flying Bull Lane School. All the people down there are tiny, like earwigs. I bet they don't know I'm up here watching. The cars are like toy cars and it feels like I'm a king in my tower. I could reach out and touch the sky.

'What's that blue stuff glinting over there?' I ask Prudence.

'It's waves. I told you we could see the sea.'

I take a great, big lungful of air. It's magic; it's even stopped raining. And there's a brilliant rainbow curving over some dark, faraway hills.

'Great up here, isn't it?' says Prudence and she

turns to me and gives me a huge, friendly grin, from one Blezzard to another.

I was grinning too and feeling on top of the world. But suddenly I'm on my guard. I swap my happy face for my bored one. 'S'all right,' I say shrugging.

'This is the storm hatch,' says Prudence. 'It's where the miller climbed out.'

I look at the long, long drop to the ground, then look quickly away. It makes me dizzy. The thought of climbing out there makes me feel sick. 'What did the miller want to climb out there for?'

'To mend the sails, of course,' says Prudence, as if she can't believe I need to ask.

I've got more questions but I bite them back. Only a Blezzard would want to know more about windmills. And I'm not a Blezzard, I'm a Trill, even though I've got miller's thumbs.

Prudence bangs the storm hatch shut. We climb down out of the cap and we're standing beside the beam with *Noah Blezzard 1805* carved on it, when she suddenly asks me, 'Is your mum going to work this mill?'

'What?' I'm shocked by her question. ''Course she isn't. She doesn't know how to work mills. And anyway, who wants windmills these days? My dad says they belong in museums –'

Suddenly we're sneezing and coughing like mad. Lots of sparkling dust comes swirling down – a whole heap of it, just dumped on our heads. We look like ghosts, we have to shake it out of our hair.

'*Achoo!* Where did that come from?' says Prudence, peering up into the cap.

But now the storm hatch is closed you can't see much. Just dark shapes and shadows. You know it's up there – all that machinery squashed into the dome. But you can't really make it out. You can't tell what's going on up there.

Slowly, the dust settles. Everything's really hushed and still. As if someone's listening.

I've got that creepy feeling again. I take a quick look over my shoulder. I want to get out of here, it doesn't feel safe.

'Let's go,' I tell Prudence. 'My mum will be wondering where I am.'

She nods, 'All right,' and we start climbing

back down.

When we get to the stone floor, I feel a bit better. It's light and I can see the world outside, through the windows.

There's Dad down there, unloading shopping from the back of the car. A frozen pizza (ham and pineapple) falls out his carrier bag and he bends down to pick it up. When he looks up again I wave but he doesn't see me. It's as if I'm invisible. As if I've been taken out of the real world and put in some kind of parallel universe.

'Yeah, Dad's going to clear this whole place out,' I tell Prudence in a loud, defiant voice, trying to make myself feel brave. 'He's going to get rid of all this junk, all this old machinery.' I sweep my arm round the stone floor. 'He's going to put his computers and fax machines in here. It'll be class, won't it?'

There's a creaking sound. Just a very tiny one from somewhere in the gear wheels, way above our heads. And the floor underneath us starts vibrating. Like something's stirring, coming to life.

'Hey,' I shout out in alarm. 'I thought you said there was no power in this mill. I mean, it's like, *dead*, isn't it? I thought you said the sails couldn't go round?'

'They can't. The brake's on.'

Prudence doesn't look scared. She's uncool and dressed like a scarecrow. But, you've got to admit, she doesn't get easily scared. Except that now she's chewing the cuffs of her woolly jumpers. So maybe she is just a *tiny* bit worried.

Then, just beyond the millstones, something rattles in the shadows. Our eyes shoot towards it. It's the silver sack hoist chain. Bit by bit, it comes jerking up through the hole in the trapdoor. We just stare and stare, as if we're hypnotized by it.

'What's getting pulled up?' That's what I'm thinking. And I bet Prudence is too.

What's coming up through that trapdoor?

CHAPTER 4

Windmills in the blood

Clank, clank – that chain's still jangling up.

Whatever's coming up on the chain will push the trapdoor open. Any second now –

'It'll be a sack, stupid.' I try reassuring myself. Just a sack of corn, that's all.

'Why is it working?' I ask Prudence in a trembling whisper. 'There's no power in the mill.'

'You can work the hoist without wind power. You can work it by hand from the bin floor or the cap floor, by turning a handle,' whispers Prudence. Even Prudence is whispering now.

I glance fearfully upwards. 'But we've just come from those floors. I didn't see anyone up there, did you?'

Frowning, she shakes her head.

Clank, clank.

Every nerve in my body is quivering, just waiting for that trapdoor to fly open.

Clank, clank. Then – silence.

One last rattle and the chain stops, as suddenly as it started.

'Pheeeew.' I let the air out my lungs in a long gasp. I didn't even realize I was holding my breath.

We listen, our ears alert for any sound. But the whole mill is deathly quiet. The white dust lies thick and still. Suddenly I notice how warm it is in here and how sweet it smells. A strange, sweet smell.

There's nothing to hear but our own hearts thumping.

Prudence Blezzard and I look at each other.

'Come on, let's get out of here.'

I forget to whisper and my voice echoes in and out of the dark machinery. *'Out of here, out of here.'* I go crashing down the stairs to the ground floor, trampling over sacks to get to the door that lets us out.

Next thing I know, I'm lying on the grass outside, looking up at the black mill tower. It seems to be leaning, just about to topple and crush me. The shadow of its sails falls over me like a crooked cross. I roll over quickly until I'm out of its shadow and in bright sunlight.

Then I sit up.

The first thing I see is Prudence Blezzard striding off in her wellies. She's already passed the mill house. She must be going home to High Cold Knott Farm.

'Hey!' I shout after her. 'I thought you were coming for tea.'

She turns round. She's got a grim, determined look on her face. 'I got to go home,' she says, 'to see our Noah. I got to ask him something.'

I watch her stomping up a track that's spiky with brambles. She looks like a North Pole Explorer in all those clothes.

You wouldn't think I'd be bothered, because I've already decided she's only a *temporary* friend. But a tiny, desperate voice inside me is begging her: 'Please stay a bit longer.'

I need a windmill expert to tell me what on earth's going on. I need someone clear-headed and calm, like Prudence Blezzard, to help me unscramble my brain.

But then another voice butts in and says, 'Don't be a weed, Trill. You don't need her. You don't need any freaky Blezzards hanging around.'

I get up, stuff my miller's thumbs deep in my pocket and walk out between the shadow of the sails.

The first thing I say when I go bursting into the mill house is, 'Mum? Can I still have that operation?'

She isn't baking cakes for tea. She's working on the computer, printing some stuff out. She looks up, frowning. 'Why, did somebody tease you about your hand?'

'No, there was another kid there – a girl with a hand just like mine.' I can't help sounding resentful.

'Well, that's good isn't it?' says Mum. 'So you found a friend? I told you, didn't I? I told you some of the Blezzards had two thumbs on their right hands.'

'No, you never told me that.'

'I most certainly did.'

'No, you didn't.'

I can't remember her telling me that. But I probably wasn't listening. If I'd heard her I would have remembered. I would have been *prepared*.

'Who was this girl?'

'Prudence Blezzard,' I tell her scowling. 'I had to sit next to her all day and she's the last kid I'd have chosen. It was embarrassing. She's –'

'She's related to us,' interrupted my mum. 'They live on the farm up the track. They're third cousins once removed or something. I can never work it out. But we're definitely related. Once a Blezzard, always a Blezzard.'

I can't believe my ears. My own mum is speaking their language.

'What, Mum? What did you just say?'

'I said, "Once a Blezzard, always a Blezzard." It's what folks say round here.'

'For heaven's sake, Mum. What are you saying things like that for? You never used to talk like that.'

'Like what?'

'Like – like *they* do.'

I'm in a bad temper now. There's no escape from Blezzards. Even the pub in the village is named after them.

'Anyway,' says Mum, closing down the computer. 'I think it's really *nice* that Prudence is your friend.'

'I don't want her to be my friend!' I yell at Mum. 'There was this really cool kid with hundred pound trainers who was nearly my friend. Until he found out I was one of those Blezzards. Then he didn't want to know me!'

'What?' says Mum. 'What are you raving about? Look, why didn't you invite Prudence for tea? After all, us Blezzards should stick together.'

It's the last straw.

'*Grrrr.*' I'm shaking my head, making my hands into fists and growling like an angry bear. I do that sometimes. When I've had enough, when I've run out of words and I just can't *stand* any more, that growl comes bursting out. '*Grrrrr.*'

'Now, don't fly off the handle, Simon,' says

Mum in her soothing voice. 'Don't get in one of your moods.'

That just makes me worse.

I crash a few doors and stomp up to my bedroom. But not before I've microwaved two boxes of crinkly chips to take up there with me. Two and a half minutes on high.

So I'm up in my bedroom guzzling hot chips and gradually calming myself down, when suddenly I freeze with a chip half-way to my mouth.

'Clang, clang, clang.'

The alarm bell on my bedroom wall is ringing.

I didn't think it worked any more. I didn't think the wires were connected up. But they must be. Or it wouldn't be ringing, would it?

'Clang, clang.' There it goes again. It sounds really urgent.

Then it stops.

I jump off the bed. My chips fly all over the place.

'Mum! Mum!' I go clattering down the stairs.

'Mum, that bell in my bedroom just rang.'

Mum smiles and shakes her head: 'It couldn't have.'

'It did. It did! Didn't you hear it?'

'It couldn't have, Simon. That bell is to tell the miller that the hopper is nearly empty. It rings automatically when the grain level gets low. If the miller's over here and there's no one in the mill then he'd better get back there double-quick. Because if the stones are running with no grain between them they could make sparks. The whole mill would go up in flames.'

'But it did ring. Honest. I'm not making it up.'

I can feel a growl swelling up inside me. I'm getting frantic again. Why won't she believe me?

'The alarm system only works when the mill's running,' Mum insists. 'And the mill's not running is it? It can't run. It's shut down; the brake's on. Look, the sails aren't turning, are they?'

I peer out of the kitchen window. We're right beside the mill. The sails sweep over the roof of our house. But they're not sweeping now. They're still.

'You don't need to look,' says Mum. 'When the sails are turning you can hear them. They make a lovely sound, *swoosh, swoosh,* when they go round, like swans flying over.'

Oh no, she's getting all poetic about windmills. She's got that same dreamy look in her eyes as Prudence – as if she can see our mill working inside her head.

I want to ask her, 'How do you know so much about windmills?' But I daren't. What if she starts spouting Blezzard-speak at me? What if she says, 'Us Blezzards are *born* knowing about windmills. Windmills are in our blood'?

Then an awful thing happens. My right hand is stuffed in my pocket, safely out of the way. But my miller's thumbs are twitching! I try to ignore them. But I can't. They're jumping like they're getting electric shocks. I can even *hear* them – a rustly sound like grasshoppers' legs. I know what they're doing in there! They're rubbing against my fingers. Just like a miller does when he tests the flour.

I make a sort of strangled noise: *'Aaaargh.'*

Then I clench my fist and hook my four fingers over those miller's thumbs. They're trapped; they can't move. So they've got to behave themselves now.

'Give me six,' says Mum, grinning.

But, for the first time ever in front of Mum, I keep my right hand hidden in my pocket.

Mum shrugs and looks worried. 'Tomorrow will be better,' she says. 'It's tough starting a new school.'

'Where's Dad?' I ask her. Suddenly I want to see my dad. Dad's really sensible. He's a Trill. And us Trills have got to stick together.

'Dad's in the study doing some work. Don't disturb him.'

'Huh.'

I go stamping back upstairs. I sit on my bed, watching that bell and trying to think things out.

The wire from the bell goes through the wall of our house, then through the wall of the mill on the stone floor. Then it goes to the hopper.

But that bell can only work when the rest of the machinery's working.

Unless somebody or *something* in the mill pulled that wire by hand.

What if that cool kid is right? What if Blezzard's Mill is haunted?

I have to tell myself off: 'Stop it. Stop it, Simon. That's enough thinking about windmills. You've got windmills on the brain.'

'And in your blood,' a tiny voice whispers inside my head. 'You've got windmills in your blood.'

My right hand has sneaked out my pocket, like a big pink spider crawling out of its den. I scowl at my thumbs. We're not friends any more. They make me nervous – I don't trust them. Any second now, they might start rubbing together, like they're testing flour. I jam them tightly between my knees.

'Get out of that,' I tell them.

It hurts a lot actually, because my knees are quite sharp and bony and they're crushing my hand really hard. But I don't care about the pain. At least those miller's thumbs know who's boss.

CHAPTER 5

Noah

Something just woke me up. What was it? My brain's still woozy. Everything's fuzzy and grey. It must be early, I'm still not properly awake yet.

What's that jingling noise in my head? It's giving me a terrible headache –

Suddenly, *snap*, I'm wide awake. I've just realized what woke me up. The alarm bell from the mill is ringing.

Clank, clank, clank – the clapper's rattling like mad inside the bell. I can see the wire tugging it.

Why can't Mum and Dad hear it? It sounds like I've got a steel band in here.

Maybe it's a message for me alone. It's as if the bell's ordering me, 'Get over here, quick!' But I'm not going. Oh no. Do you think I'm stupid? Like one of those kids in films who go *exploring* in haunted houses? Who say, 'I wonder what's down in that dark, creepy cellar?' Or 'I wonder what's behind this locked door?' They deserve what they get.

I'm staying here, snuggled up warm in my duvet. It can ring as much as it likes.

Oh no! My thumbs on my right hand, my *miller's* thumbs, are twitching away, like those sticks that search for water. They seem really excited about something!

'Hey, stop it. Stop messing about!' I yell at my thumbs.

What's going on? My thumbs never behaved like this in our old house. They never gave me any trouble at all.

I'm lying there petrified, wondering what on earth to do next. When, suddenly, without any warning, the bell stops.

Instantly, my thumbs stop misbehaving. They're not twitchy any more. They're as floppy as dead slugs.

But I'm still shaking. I'm thinking, 'This can't be happening – bells ringing, my thumbs going berserk!'

Maybe I'm still dreaming. But when I give my right hand a vicious squeeze, it hurts a lot. 'Ow.'

So I can't be dreaming, can I?

I crawl out of bed. I can see Blezzard's Mill through a gap in my curtains. The tips of two sails have a rosy glow where the rising sun's hit them. But the rest of the mill tower has grey mist swirling round it.

What's that, moving up there on the cap? My eyes are drawn to it. I don't want to look but I can't look away.

The storm hatch is opening.

I feel freezing cold, then sick and hot. A ghostly figure is climbing out of the storm hatch onto a sail. It clings there, hanging onto the open shutter. Then it starts moving up the sail, just like it's climbing a ladder.

Where's it gone? The mist has swallowed it up.

For a while I can't see it at all. But it must be

still climbing. Because in a minute I make out a head, rising out of the mist into the clear, pink light of dawn. The head hasn't got any hair. It's white and bald as a mushroom.

The thing on the sail stops climbing, with only its head showing above the mist. The mushroom head starts to turn. Its face is fungus-white. It turns until it's staring with black eye holes straight down at me –

I yank my curtains shut, stagger back to my bed and crash down on my duvet. But I'm trembling with panic, I can't stay still. So I leap up again and drag my computer chair across the floor. When it's under the bell I climb onto it and try to rip out the wire.

'Ouch!' It slices my right hand like a razor. I can't rip it loose. I need wire cutting tools or something. I run back to the window.

'Look,' I dare myself. 'Go on, look.'

Taking a deep breath, I yank back the curtain.

The mist has gone. Now the whole mill is glowing red with the dawn, as if it's on fire. There's no one on the sails. And the storm hatch is closed up again.

I don't know what to think. I daren't think at all. I can only make grizzly bear noises, *'Grrrrrrrr,'* and shake my head hopelessly.

Downstairs Mum says, 'You're up early.' When I put on my coat she says, 'It's too early to go to school.'

'I'm going to meet Prudence Blezzard,' I tell her.

'Oh, your new friend,' she says, looking pleased.

'Grrrr,' I'm thinking, inside my head.

'What about breakfast?' says Mum.

I slap a peanut butter sandwich together and start wolfing it down. I'm not going to meet Prudence Blezzard. She's the last person I want to see – with her scarecrow clothes and her cow-splat wellies and her calm, moon-face and her miller's thumbs. No, I'm going to keep right away from her, I swear I am. I'm going to stick with *normal* kids. Then maybe all these awful, scary things will stop happening.

And if anyone says I'm a Blezzard, or if anyone says I've got windmills in my blood – I'm going to punch them in the nose.

'What's wrong with your hand?' asks Mum.

'I cut it.'

Mum looks really shocked and upset and suddenly I can guess what she's thinking. She's thinking, 'Simon hasn't tried to cut his spare thumb off, has he?'

I could tell her it was only an accident, that I wasn't trying to be a do-it-yourself surgeon. But I don't *feel* like telling her. I've just been scared out of my wits. I'm still scared. And being scared makes me angry and cruel.

'I want that operation, right?' is all I say, as I go stomping towards the door.

'Right?' I snarl again as I crash out of the house with my hand screwed deep in my pocket. Bet Mum worries about me all day now. I feel a sharp twist of guilt about that. But I don't turn back.

I trudge, head down, past the windmill. I daren't look up – I'm terrified of what I might see.

It's still too early to go to school but I walk down to the village. Where else is there to go?

At least my thumbs are quiet now. They're being good, not even tingling.

'Get a grip, Simon,' I tell myself, sternly. 'Be sensible, like a Trill.' The Trills are well-known for being sensible. They're famous for it. My dad's the most sensible person in the world, the galaxy, the universe.

What's that purple and green splodge in the distance? It's Prudence, in one of her horrible jumpers. What's she doing down here so early? Oh no, she's coming this way!

I'm desperate to avoid her. So desperate that I duck through the gates into the churchyard. The path is squidgy with wet moss. The graves smell of mould.

Then I'm round the back of the church and suddenly, the stained glass window lights up like a sunburst. It's glowing in glorious colours, blue and red and green.

But it has an awful effect on me. I forget I'm a Trill. I forget to be sensible and get a grip.

It's him, in the window! There's Blezzard's Mill and there's a tiny figure. His head is round and bald. He looks like a glass gingerbread man.

'It's *mushroom head!*' I can hardly get the words out, my voice is shaking so much with

shock and horror.

Prudence has suddenly appeared beside me. 'What are you doing in here –' she starts saying.

But I'm not listening. I don't even remember that I've just sworn to keep away from her.

Because *he's there*. Climbing like a monkey up one of the sails. Just like he was this morning.

'I saw him,' I gasp. 'The alarm bell in my bedroom rang and then it stopped. Then I looked outside and *he* was there. He climbed out of the storm hatch and went up the sails. Like he's doing in that window.'

'Are you *sure* it was him?' asks Prudence.

Even she sounds a bit rattled.

'Because that's Noah Blezzard,' she says. 'He's the one whose name is carved in the mill. Remember I showed you? He's been dead since 1812. In fact, you're standing right on top of him.'

CHAPTER 6

A real live ghost

'Aaaaargh!'

I do a great, froggy leap sidewards, then spin around.

I've been standing on a mossy grave. It's got a millwheel for a headstone. And round the edge of the millwheel are some words.

I can't seem to read them. I slap my head, *whop*, to clear it but my brain's gone on strike. It just can't cope with what's happening. Prudence crouches down to read the words for me.

'NOAH BLEZZARD, LOST HIS LIFE FROM A WINDMILL, Jan 12th, 1812. AGED 61 YEARS.

DEATH CAME SUDDEN.'

'What's it mean?' I ask Prudence, still in a daze. 'What's it mean, "DEATH CAME SUDDEN"?'

'Don't you know about him?' she says, surprised. 'I thought all us Blezzards knew that story. It's family history.'

'For heaven's sake!' I'd have gritted my teeth if they weren't chattering so much.

A cloud hides the sun. Suddenly, it's so damp and cold and creepy in the churchyard I have to hug myself to stop the shakes. The stained glass window's gone black, like a telly screen switched off. You can't see Blezzard's Mill any more, or the little old man on the sails.

'Forget about all this Blezzard family history stuff,' I beg Prudence. 'Just tell me the story. All right?'

But while my mouth is saying this, my brain is gabbling at me, 'You saw a ghost this morning. A real live ghost.'

I mean, a real dead one.

'Well, Noah Blezzard was old, see,' says Prudence, pointing to the sixty-one on the millstone. 'And he was out trying to mend the sails and he fell off. The sails started turning like this –'

As she's telling me this bit, Prudence's right arm is sweeping round in big, wide circles. She's so sparky and excited when she's talking about windmills. She really brings windmills to life.

'He managed to hang on for a bit. He went round and round with the sails. Round and round, shouting for help, but there was no one there. But then the cap turned the sails into the wind's eye. And the sails started going faster and faster.' Prudence's arm is whirling like a helicopter now. 'And he couldn't keep hold and he got thrown off and smashed to pieces on the ground – it's a mystery really. Because the mill shouldn't have been working. I mean, he'd been a windmiller all his life.

He wouldn't have climbed out onto the sails without putting the brake on. He'd never do that.

So nobody knows what really happened. Maybe the brake slipped off or something.'

I gulp two or three times. I've got to face the

truth. I don't want to, but what other explanation is there?

'Prudence?'

'Yes?'

'I saw a ghost this morning, didn't I? I saw the ghost of Noah Blezzard. You hear about it all the time, ghosts haunting the places where they met *violent* deaths. Well, he's doing that, isn't he? That cool kid was right. There's a ghost in Blezzard's Mill.'

It all adds up. Bells ringing, chains rattling – spooks do that kind of thing. You read about it all the time.

I've made up my mind. 'I'm not going back into that mill again,' I tell Prudence. I wish we'd never come here. I wish we were back where we used to live, a hundred miles away from Blezzard's Mill.

She sighs and shakes her head.

'Look, Simon –' she starts off in a soothing voice as if she's talking to a crazy person.

'Don't you believe me? You don't believe me, do you, that I saw him on the sails? You think I'm making it all up!'

I'm yelling at Prudence, right into her face. I'm scared, really scared. And that makes me lose my cool.

'Well, I don't care,' I rave at her. 'I'm having that operation. I'm having my extra thumb cut off! And then I won't be anything like you freaky Blezzards. I'll just be a *normal* kid. And everything will be back to *normal.* And all these creepy things will stop happening!'

I go tearing out of that churchyard like Noah Blezzard has just leapt up from his grave and is chasing me. Prudence stands there, staring after me.

Just inside the school gates, I crash into cool kid in his silver trainers.

'Give me six,' he says, lifting his hand high. He's trying to be friendly.

But I'm not going to give him six. No way, I daren't risk it. Those miller's thumbs are far too dangerous to let out of my coat pocket.

So I just cut him dead and walk away. He looks after me with his mouth hanging open. He can't believe it. A popular kid like him isn't used to being ignored.

'Did you see that?' he's telling everyone, in a loud voice. 'I should have known. You can't make friends with that lot. They're weird. I thought he might be different but he isn't. Once a Blezzard always a Blezzard.'

During Maths lesson, cool kid keeps shooting me deadly looks across the classroom. He's still mad at me because I wouldn't give him six.

Prudence isn't talking to me either. She's staring out of the window, lost in her own thoughts. I don't care. I don't want to talk to her anyway. I wish I didn't have to sit next to her. I wish this classroom was a Blezzard-free zone.

I feel like wearing a big badge that says: I'M A TRILL. OK? so there's no mistake.

Those pesky miller's thumbs are acting up again. I can feel them twitching, burrowing away like moles in my pocket. I hate them. They're like a family curse. They let the whole world know that I come from a long line of windmill freaks.

'Stop it,' I hiss at them. '*Please*, stop it.'

I think I'm going crazy. I'm a quivering wreck. I'm talking to my own thumbs!

'Get a grip, Trill,' I warn myself, in my most sarcastic tone of voice.

I can see Blezzard's Mill out of the classroom window. It makes me tremble just to look at it. It's like a mighty, menacing robot with a swivel head, black against the sky.

At least Noah Blezzard's ghost isn't climbing up the sails.

Maybe he's inside, on the stone floor. Maybe that bell's ringing now, in my empty bedroom, calling me to the mill, where he's waiting –

'– That's what our Noah says.'

Who said that? I look around. Then I realize Prudence has been speaking to me.

For a second, I look at her blankly. It takes a real effort to drag my thoughts back to the classroom. We're supposed to be doing maths questions one to six. But I can't help noticing that like me, she hasn't even started.

'What did you say?' My voice sounds snooty and unfriendly. But I can't help that either. I mean, I'm not supposed to be talking to her *at all*, am I?

'I said, there isn't a ghost. Our Noah says so.'

I just explode.

'*Your* Noah's wrong then, isn't he! He doesn't know what he's talking about! He must be stupid!'

You can't keep anything private in a classroom, can you? Some nosey parker from the next table's been listening. Because he suddenly interrupts and says, 'Huh! You'd better not call their Noah stupid. He's really tough. He's been in loads of trouble. He's the toughest kid around here.'

'How would I know that?' I tell him. 'I haven't even seen him.'

When I say that, Prudence looks a bit shifty. Which is strange because she isn't a shifty person. 'Our Noah doesn't mix with people much,' she says. 'He doesn't like people. He only likes windmills.'

'Don't tell me he's got windmills in his blood?'

'More than any of us Blezzards,' says Prudence. 'He's got them in his blood. And on the brain too. Windmills matter more to our Noah than anything else in the world.'

'Oh great,' I mutter gloomily. 'Another windmill freak is all I need. Just keep him away from me, that's all.'

My life these days – it's just one problem after another.

'Simon Trill!' says Miss, from the front of the class. 'I don't know how you behaved at your last school. But at Flying Bull Lane School, we keep our heads down and *work*.'

Like I said, one problem after another.

CHAPTER 7

On the cap floor

After school Prudence asks me, out of the blue, 'Want to come to my house for tea?'

I glance sneakily round to see if that cool kid can hear us. But he's nowhere in sight.

I don't want to go to High Cold Knott Farm with Prudence. And what about Prudence's hard-man brother, Noah? What if he's heard that I called him stupid?

But I don't want to go home to Blezzard's Mill either. Where alarm bells ring in my bedroom and spooks stare at me from windmill sails.

Isn't anywhere safe? Maybe I'll just stay here,

at Flying Bull Lane School. But I don't want to be left all on my own, in an empty school. I used to have nightmares about that when I was little.

It's cold and I've got to go *somewhere*. So I shrug reluctantly and tell Prudence, 'OK then.' We go trudging through the village, past The Miller's Thumbs pub. At least we're not taking the short cut through the churchyard. I don't want to read Noah Blezzard's gravestone, 'DEATH CAME SUDDEN' or see his baldy mushroom head sparkling in the stained glass window.

I wonder if I'll see him again tonight? I wonder if the bell will ring and my thumbs will start acting up? My skin's crawling just *thinking* about it.

'You'd better not start jumping around!' I warn my miller's thumbs.

'Course, I don't talk to them out loud. I do it privately, inside my head. I don't want the whole world to think I'm nuts.

Prudence is saying something to me. At first I'm not listening. But when I *do* listen, my mouth just falls wide open. Have you seen how egg-swallowing snakes look when they unhinge their jaws? I look like that.

'Actually,' Prudence is telling me, 'I want to go into Blezzard's Mill. And I want you to come with me.'

I was fairly frantic before. But I'm in panic mode now. My brain is screaming at me: 'Red alert! Red alert!'

I start protesting: 'I thought we were going to your house!'

'It won't take long,' she says. She sounds really cool and determined. As if she's planned all this beforehand. We're already in the shadow of the mill's sails.

'I'm not going up there! No way. Noah Blezzard's ghost is in there. It's a horrible mushroom-head with black holes for eyes. And it doesn't like me. You ought to have seen the way it glared at me this morning. You must be out of your mind if you think I'm going in there. I'm *never* going in there.'

Prudence waits patiently until I've stopped ranting and raving.

Then she says, in a quiet voice, 'Well, I am.'

She flicks her plaits over her back, pulls her tea-cosy hat down low on her head and disappears inside.

She doesn't close the door behind her, so I can hear her welly boots clumping up the wooden stairs. Then I can't hear anything else. Just silence.

I'm imagining it inside the mill. The stone floor, then the bin floor, then the cap floor right at the top. Dusty and silent and crammed with machinery. All the spooky, shadowy corners where things could hide and spring out at you.

'I'm not going in there,' I tell myself, shaking my head so hard that my brain rattles. 'Absolutely *no* way.'

What's Prudence doing? She's been gone for ages.

I wait a bit more, hopping about from one foot to the other.

She's been gone even longer now. I can't hear a single squeak from inside Blezzard's Mill. It's as if time has stopped.

Should I go in after her?

I haven't got much choice, have I? Well, I have. I could run away. But my pride won't let me. And besides, I can hardly turn up at High Cold Knott Farm without her, can I? I can hardly say, 'Hi everybody! I've come for tea. And, by the way, I've left Prudence in Blezzard's Mill with a ghost.'

I already know what they'd say. They'd say, 'How could you? Us Blezzards should stick together.'

I'm still arguing with myself: 'Should I? Shouldn't I?' when suddenly there's a crash. It

sounds faint
and far away,
somewhere
high up inside the mill.

'Prudence?'

I've stopped thinking now. I'm just running.
Running into the mill, clattering up the wooden
steps. There's a gleam of silver – it's the sack
hoist chain. Then I'm up where the millstones
are, with the wooden wheels, beams and shafts
all round me. And, all the time, my eyes are
darting around – in case that
mushroom-head is crouched in
some gloomy corner.

'Prudence?'

No answer. It's as if
Blezzard's Mill has swallowed
her up.

Some silvery dust drifts
down. I look up, scared. But it's
stopped already. There's total
stillness.

Where is she? She must be up on the bin
floor. The wooden stairs creak when I tread on

them. 'Whossat?' It makes me jump out of my skin.

But there's no one on the bin floor either. The sack hoist chain isn't rattling. The dust isn't blowing about. There's one big HUSH.

But it makes me feel jumpier than ever. Because it's not a nice, restful hush. I don't like it. It's eerie; spine-tingling. As if something is waiting to happen.

I've got to go higher. There's only one place left for Prudence to be – the cap floor.

Creak. Every creaky step makes me stop, hold my breath and listen – and when nothing happens I go up one more step.

I'm on the cap floor now.

It's like a twilight world up here. The storm hatch isn't open. It's hard to make things out. What's that?

What's that dark shape, creeping around the walls? What is it?

My guts are slopping around inside me. But my brain is ready to explode –

'HELLO!' booms Prudence, looming up out the shadows. 'It's only me.'

'You idiot! Stop messing about!'

I'm shaky and sick with relief. I thought she was the ghost. I really did. I'm mad too because I feel such a fool. 'I came rushing up,' I tell Prudence in an accusing voice. 'I heard a noise. I thought something awful had happened to you.'

'I tripped over,' is all Prudence says. Her voice sounds steady, not like mine. But she's looking upwards, into the white dome, where all the massive clockwork wheels are packed in tight.

A little trickle of dust comes floating down.

I stare upwards too. 'What can you see?'

'Oh, nothing,' says Prudence. But her eyes are still flickering about.

I'm still really nervous. And when I get nervous I get uncool. I talk a lot, in a very high voice.

'My dad is going to clear all that junk out,' I tell her. 'All that junk up there in the cap. He says it's useless old machinery. He won't even get any money for it. Except, he says, you could probably sell the millstones for garden ornaments and – wait a minute, whose are those?'

I've just spotted some strange bootprints in the dust. Ghosts don't leave bootprints do they? But just as I'm kneeling to look, there's a clattering noise above our heads. My eyes shoot upwards.

'Watch out!' yells Prudence, knocking me out the way with a mighty shove.

I go sprawling onto the floor. There are clouds of dust all around me blinding me, making me cough. Then there's a dreadful, thundering *KERRASH!* that makes the floor shake. Something's just hurtled down from the cap. I try to get up but it's crouching beside me. A monster with big boots and a white, shiny head like a skull. He's shouting at me out of his roaring face.

A shockwave shoots through my body. I fall backwards. Then I point a trembling finger and start yelling too. 'It's *him*. It's *him*. It's the ghost. It's Noah Blezzard!'

'You could've hurt someone just then,' says Prudence to the ghost.

Why isn't she as panicky as I am? Why isn't she scared out of her mind? She even sounds as if she's telling it off. What's going on? I look at her, then back at the ghost.

He's stopped shouting. His face is thin and deathly pale. There are black stains under his eyes like bruises. But I can see now that he's no old man's ghost. He's a boy, about sixteen. He's as alive as I am.

But don't think I'm relaxed. Oh no. Because this boy looks mean. It's that shaved head, those glinty eyes in a rock-hard face. He's got knee-high, laced up boots and an eyebrow full of rings. And miller's thumbs.

I know who he is. He's Prudence's brother. The one who doesn't like people. The one who thinks that windmills are the most important thing in the universe.

'Tell him, Noah,' begs Prudence. 'Tell Simon there isn't any ghost. That it was you all the time.'

Noah grins. It's a little twisted grin. 'You never saw me, did you?' He sounds really proud. 'I was up there.' He jerks his miller's thumbs towards the cap. 'I was lying along the windshaft watching you. Listening to everything you said. I chucked some dust down at you. But you never saw me, did you?'

He's saying all this to Prudence. He's ignoring me, as if I don't exist.

But I want to make a hundred per cent sure there's no ghost in this mill, so I blurt out, before I can stop myself, 'It was you on the sails this morning, wasn't it? It was you who tugged on the sack hoist chain?' I'm just going to say, 'And you rang the bell in my bedroom didn't you?'

but before I can get the words out, he whirls round, ferociously. His eyes go wide and amazed as if he's saying, 'You talking to ME?'

He darts me another savage look and snarls at me, like a wolf, showing all his sharp teeth.

Then he pounds down the stairs. We can hear his big boots, clattering all the way down to the bin floor, then the stone floor. A few moments later, the windmill door slams.

He's gone.

The mill is silent again. Prudence and I just stand there, staring at each other. The only thing I can do is say, '*Phew,*' and wipe the sweat off my forehead. I can't seem to find any words.

Then Prudence says, 'I thought it was Noah. He was trying to frighten you off. There isn't any ghost. It was only our Noah.'

'*Phew.* I'm really glad this mill's not haunted.' But I'm not as glad as all that. Because, if I had a choice between having their Noah in the mill, or the ghost of some old miller – then I'd probably choose the ghost. He'd be a lot less scary.

CHAPTER 8

Like swans, flying over

On our way past the mill house, Mum beckons us from the kitchen window. She comes to the back door to meet us.

'Who was that I saw running out of the mill just now?' she asks me.

'*Errrrr*,' I mumble, playing for time. I don't know whether to tell her or not.

But Prudence comes straight out with it. 'It was our Noah,' she tells Mum. She sounds embarrassed.

'Ahhh,' says Mum, looking thoughtful. 'And you're Prudence, aren't you? You live at the farm?'

Prudence nods.

'I've seen your brother round our mill before,' she tells Prudence. 'He comes here a lot, doesn't he?'

Prudence looks even more embarrassed. She starts chewing the cuffs of her jumper until the purple wool is all raggy. She shuffles her wellies about. Then, at last, when I think she's never going to answer, she bursts out, 'I know he shouldn't. I know it's your mill now. But he's not doing any harm. He's only trying to look after it. He loves this mill. He really cares about it. You know your cousin who left you the mill? Noah helped him to run it. He knows all about windmills. He could run this mill himself. He knows how all the machinery works.'

I think Prudence expects my mum to be angry. But Mum says, 'He wants the mill to keep working, doesn't he?'

Prudence looks really surprised that my mum knows this. But I'm not surprised. Mum was a teacher before we came here. She taught some big, tough kids, as tough as Noah. She wasn't scared of them. She knew all sorts of things about them.

Knowing Mum understands makes Prudence a lot more confident. I've never heard her talk so much before. 'Our Noah was in a lot of trouble,' she explains to Mum. 'With the police and everything. He was a bad lad, everyone said so. But when he was allowed to help in the mill, he just loved it. He didn't get into no more trouble. He says –' Prudence stops talking and flicks her plaits about and chews on her cuffs a bit more. As if she can't decide whether to carry on or not.

'What does he say?' asks Mum gently.

'Noah says – he says that he *talks* to the mill. He says he loves all the sounds it makes when it's working. It's like it's alive. The millstones rumble and the sack chain rattles. And the sails go *swoosh, swoosh*. Like swans flying over, Noah says.'

Mum's eyes are going all soft and dreamy. She's getting that windmill look. 'You said that, about the swans,' I remind her.

But she doesn't need reminding. And, somehow, I can read her mind. I know just what she's imagining. She's got a vision of Blezzard's Mill in her head – of the mill working. With all the wheels in its brain-box whirring round. And the sails swishing like great, white, angel's wings. And the machinery turning as smooth as cream, and purring like a happy cat.

Oh no. What am I doing? I'm having that vision too. And those miller's thumbs are getting all excited, rubbing my fingers like big chirruping crickets. As if they can't wait to start testing the flour.

'Stop it. Stop doing that,' I tell my miller's thumbs. I tangle them up with my fingers so they're in a big, wormy knot. That'll fix 'em – for a while.

I said, 'Stop it,' out loud. Not secretly inside my head. I must have done, because Prudence and Mum are looking at me *very* strangely.

Then Mum says, 'I've been thinking a lot

about my windmill.'

She looks past my shoulder. All three of us gaze at the black tower with its huge, sweeping sails and the white dome on the top. It's breathtaking. Majestic. I've got to admit it. Even I think so. And I don't like windmills, do I?

'I've been thinking that it'd be a terrible shame to shut it down, to make it into an office,' says Mum.

'Honest?' I'm really surprised. 'I thought it was already decided?'

'Well, it was,' says Mum. 'It seemed the most *sensible* thing to do, you know, for your dad's business. But when I came back to Blezzard's Mill, I started remembering things. How long this mill's been in our family, for instance. Nearly two hundred years. And all that time it's been a working mill. How I came here when I was a little girl. It smelled sweet in there, you know. A lovely, warm, sweet smell, like someone making toffee.'

'That's the barley meal,' Prudence says eagerly. 'Noah told me about that. It smells sweet when they grind up barley meal.'

Oh dear, they're both getting dreamy now.

Mum shakes herself, like a dog coming out of a stream. Then she says, in a business-like voice, 'Anyhow, I've been *seriously* thinking about keeping it running.'

Prudence clasps her hands together, as if she's thrilled to bits. 'That's great,' she says. 'I *knew* you'd keep the mill working. I just *knew* it. Once a Blezzard, always a Blezzard.'

'That's right,' grins Mum.

This time I don't even raise my eyebrows. What's the use? I'm outnumbered.

Prudence hesitates. Then she asks Mum, 'Can I tell our Noah?'

'He's mad at us,' I explain to Mum. 'He's really mad because he thinks we're closing it down.'

'I know,' Mum says. 'I think he's very bitter. He hates our guts.'

Don't ask me how she knows. She just knows these things.

'Can I tell him then?' asks Prudence.

Mum frowns. Then says, as if she's made an important decision, 'You can tell him that I want to keep it open. I can't promise. But I'll try my best to find a way of doing it. Tell him that. OK?'

Prudence gives a solemn nod.

Then Mum smiles as if she's happy now she's decided. 'Give me six,' she says to Prudence.

And they slap hands and do a little dance. Honestly, sometimes it's really embarrassing. My mum behaves more like a kid than I do.

'I can't wait to tell our Noah,' grins Prudence. 'He'll be dead chuffed!'

'I like your mum,' says Prudence as we walk

up the track to High Cold Knott Farm. It doesn't surprise me. Where we lived before, all my friends liked her. Sometimes, I even suspected they liked *her* more than they liked *me*.

We walk into Prudence's kitchen. There's nobody there. But then Prudence says, 'Hello, Noah.'

I whirl around. And there's Noah in a chair, in a dark corner. He's cuddling a tiny, new-born lamb in his arms, feeding it on a bottle. It's slurping the milk like a greedy baby. Its tail is waggling like one of those furry snakes that dance on a stick.

Then Noah lifts his head. If I thought he'd gone gentle all of a sudden, I soon forget *that* idea. Because he shoots me a stare full of poison. If looks could kill, I'd be stone-dead.

Mum was right. He hates our guts.

Then Prudence says, 'Noah, guess what? Some brilliant news. Simon's mum says she's not going to close the mill down.'

Mum didn't exactly say that. She didn't make any promises. She said she'd try her best not to shut it down.

But, when I see the change in Noah's face, I decide it's safer to keep my mouth shut. Noah's face grows bright and sunny. It glows, like it's lit up from the inside.

Then, suddenly, he swaps his happy face for a hard suspicious glare. 'You're kidding me,' he says.

'No!' booms Prudence, flipping her plaits out the way. She sounds really inspired. 'Honest, Noah, Simon's mum is a true Blezzard. She's got windmills in her blood. Just like us.'

Blezzard speak. I feel left out, as usual. But it seems to do the trick. Noah puts the lamb down. It wobbles a bit. Then stands on its own four feet.

'I got to tell the mill,' says Noah.

His voice sounds choked with excitement. He

can hardly get the words out. I can't have heard him right anyway. Did he say, *'tell the mill'*? Naa, he couldn't have.

Then he says, in the same excited voice, 'When? How soon? How soon will it be grinding corn again?'

Prudence turns to me: 'I dunno. You'll have to ask Simon.'

I'm a bit worried that things seem to be rushing ahead. 'You'll have to ask my mum,' I tell Noah, nervously. I've already decided that he won't like that answer.

But he doesn't get angry. He just nods: 'OK.'

He seems in such a good mood that I forget to be scared of him. 'Hey, that was classic what you did,' I tell him before I can stop myself. 'Making that sack hoist chain work. Climbing out on the sails. Making the bell ring in my bedroom. You nearly had me believing in ghosts, you had me scared stiff, you –'

My voice sinks to a whisper, then stops altogether. Why is he staring at me like that – with those burning eyes?

He takes two steps towards me – he has to step

over the lamb to do it. He looks so fierce that I throw up my hands to protect myself. But he just growls, 'What did you say? What did you say about the bell?'

'There – there – there's a bell on the wall in my bedroom and it's connected by a wire to the hopper in the mill and – and –'

He waves a hand to shut me up. 'I already know about the bell. I know how it works. But did you say it's been *ringing*?'

'Yes, I heard it. It woke me up this morning. But what do you want to know for?' I ask him, bewildered. '*You* made it ring, didn't you? It was *you* in the mill, pulling the wire, pretending to be a ghost, making it ring?'

'You kidding me about this?' Noah's blazing eyes are searching my face, as if he's trying to find out if I'm lying. 'You wouldn't kid me about the bell, would you?'

'No, 'course not. Why should I? It was ringing like mad. It woke me up.'

'It had nothing to do with me,' he says. 'I did those other things. I wanted to scare you away, all of you! But I never went near that bell wire. Cross my heart and hope to die, it wasn't me. I never made it ring.'

CHAPTER 9

Who rang the bell?

There's a really strange look on Noah's face. I'm trying to work out what it is. I know – it's a triumphant look. Like he's going to punch the air and shout, 'Yay!' Like his team just won the cup.

'I've got to see that bell NOW,' he says, pulling at my arm as if it's really urgent. 'I want to hear it ringing.'

'You *sure* you didn't ring it?' I ask him. 'Maybe you rang it accidentally.' But he's not listening. He's already rushed out of the door.

Prudence and I just stare at each other. I

thought she might understand what was going on in Noah's head. But, this time, she looks as confused as I do.

'You coming?' Noah roars back at us from half-way across the farm yard.

'Is it all right? I mean, for our Noah to go in your house and see the bell?' asks Prudence.

I'm not thrilled about it. Their Noah makes me nervous. I don't know what he's thinking. I don't trust him. But I wouldn't dare tell him, 'No, you can't come.'

'Suppose it's all right.'

'Let's go then,' says Prudence.

'What about that lamb?'

'It's OK. Look, it's going to sleep. And anyway, Mum and Dad'll be here in a minute. They're out doing the milking.'

Noah is yelling from outside, 'Are you coming or what?'

'What's he want to see the bell for, anyway?'

'I don't know,' says Prudence, shaking her head. 'He's just crazy about the mill. He thinks about it all the time. Did you see how cheered-up he was when I told him your mum was going to save it?'

'Hummm.' I still don't like him. Even if he is cheered-up. I think he's a nutter.

I think he rang the bell from the windmill. How else could it ring?

When we get outside there's a gusty wind. Where did that come from? It really slaps us around.

'It's a good miller's wind!' Prudence yells into my ear. Honestly, can't these Blezzards ever forget about windmills?

We go staggering over the fields. But the wind doesn't stop Noah. He just lets it bounce off him. He doesn't even seem to notice. He gets to the mill house before us and for a second I think he's going to burst through the door. But he doesn't; he stops and waits.

'Come on, come on, come on,' he says when we catch up with him. He's practically foaming at the mouth with impatience. His eyes are bright and glittery like a kid who's been promised a big treat.

He doesn't even wait for me to open the back door. He opens it himself and goes clumping inside in his big boots like he owns the place.

My dad's not around. Good. My dad's a Trill through and through. He wouldn't understand Noah. I mean, Noah's not just a windmill freak. He's the freakiest windmill freak in the world, the universe. Even I'm having trouble understanding him. And I've got miller's thumbs.

They're twitching by the way. Jumping around like frisky fleas. As if they know something *big* is going to happen.

But I haven't got time to tell them off because Mum comes into the kitchen. She doesn't seem at all worried to see bad boy Noah.

Actually, I've got this awful suspicion that

Mum will get on with Noah. They've got things in common. Like getting excited about sails like swans and the sweet smell of barley meal.

Mum says, 'Hello, Prudence. Hello, Noah. How are you?'

I would have bet you a million pounds that Noah would be rude. That he'd just grunt or something.

But I'm wrong because he's really polite and respectful to Mum. He says, 'I'm all right.' Then he asks her, in a big rush of words, 'Mrs Trill, will

you let me work the mill? I can do it, honest, and you don't even have to pay me 'cos I'll do it for free –'

Mum starts to say, 'I haven't decided –'

But Noah isn't listening. His white mushroom head is tipped to one side. As if he's just heard something upstairs.

'The bell's ringing. I can hear it!' he tells us.

I can't hear a thing. What's he playing at? He's definitely round the twist.

Then Prudence tilts her head and concentrates hard. She says, 'I can hear it too.'

And, without even asking, Noah goes pounding out of our kitchen and up our stairs three at a time. 'Hey, what you doing?' I shout, racing after him. 'That's my bedroom. That's private.'

But when I get there he's opened my door and he's already inside my room. Now even I can hear the bell ringing. It's ringing frantically, *clang, clang, clang,* like someone's in distress.

Noah dashes to my window and stares out at the big, black tower of Blezzard's Mill. He pushes my window wide open.

'I can hear you!' he screams into the wind. 'It's me, Noah! I can hear you.'

'Who you talking to?' He spins round to face me, all excited. 'The mill,' he says, his eyes shining. 'Who do you think? I *knew* she listened. I could *feel* her listening. But now I know she's got a voice too. Listen to her calling me!'

A nutter, like I thought. He's talking as if he thinks the mill is alive. As if he thinks it's got a *brain*.

The bell's clanging, my thumbs are going bananas, wagging about like a two-tailed dog. Noah's yelling at the mill, 'I can hear you. I'm coming!'

For heaven's sake! Has the whole world gone mad?

Noah shoves Prudence and me out of the way: 'The mill needs me.' Then he goes clattering down the stairs. *Crash!* There goes our back door.

The bell's gone quiet. It's a while before I realize because, long after it's stopped ringing, it's still echoing in my head.

Noah's sprinting for the mill, all crouched-up like a big goblin.

Mum comes into the bedroom. 'Where's Noah going in such a hurry?'

'He said the mill *needs* him,' says Prudence.

Prudence looks really worried. I'd be worried too if that lunatic was my brother.

But my mum doesn't laugh or say, 'What a nutcase.' She looks deadly serious. She says, in a grim voice, 'I think we'd better get over there. I think there must be something wrong.' She turns to me. 'Look out the window, Simon, see where Noah's got to.'

He isn't inside the mill yet – he's stopped dead, just outside the door. And he's looking up into the sails. What can he see? His head is tipped to one side. What's he listening to?

Then we all hear it – a strange, clunking, rattling sound. I've got no idea what it is. But Prudence does. She comes rushing to the window.

'The shutters on the mill sails are closing.'

Mum pushes in at the window too: 'They can't be.'

But they are. We can all see it happening. Noah's staring upwards too. We can see every shutter snapping shut, like giant Venetian blinds being closed.

'That's impossible,' says Mum. Her voice is quiet, full of dread. 'There's no one inside the mill. You have to do that from *inside* the mill.'

'Maybe it's Dad.'

'No – he's in town. And besides, he doesn't have a clue about how windmills work.'

There's a creaking sound from somewhere outside, high up.

'Oh no.' Mum and Prudence are staring at each other. Their faces are grey with shock.

'What's the matter? Tell me what's going on,' I beg, frantically.

There's an ear-splitting *Kerrak!* Then another. I duck down, I can't help it. It sounds like the sky is ripping apart.

'The sails are turning!' cries Prudence, horrified.

115

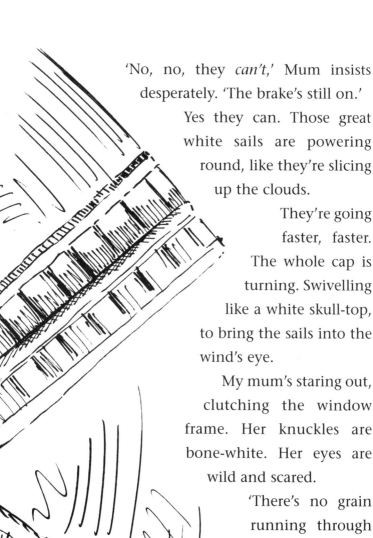

'No, no, they *can't*,' Mum insists desperately. 'The brake's still on.'

Yes they can. Those great white sails are powering round, like they're slicing up the clouds.

They're going faster, faster. The whole cap is turning. Swivelling like a white skull-top, to bring the sails into the wind's eye.

My mum's staring out, clutching the window frame. Her knuckles are bone-white. Her eyes are wild and scared.

'There's no grain running through the stones,' she's whispering, in an appalled voice. 'My mill is running empty.'

'What's that mean?' I ask Prudence. Mum told me once, but I can't remember. I can't think straight, my head's spinning, like the sails.

Prudence's eyes look straight into mine. Her eyes are terrified too, just like Mum's.

'It means the mill's out of control. If you can't stop it, it just goes faster and faster. The millstones strike sparks. It'll burn down. If it doesn't shake itself to pieces first.'

I remember now. About sails ripping off and mills cracking open. Or bursting into flames like fiery crosses.

'Come on,' says Prudence, urgently.

She's got a grim and determined look on her face. She grabs Mum's arm. My mum's in a daze, still staring out the window, as if she can't believe what her eyes are telling her.

'Where's Dad?' I ask her.

'I told you, he's not here,' Mum says, still staring at the sails. They're speeding round now like mad, whirling arms. *Swish, swish, swish.* They're slashing the sky to bits. They don't sound like swan's wings. They sound like bat's wings to me. Great, leathery bat wings, swooping round.

'Come on, Mrs Trill,' begs Prudence, tugging at Mum's arm. 'We've got to go. Your mill is destroying itself. We've got to try and stop it!'

CHAPTER 10

'We've got to stop the mill!'

We're all running towards the mill.

When we're under the sails we can feel their great power. *Whoosh, whoosh,* slicing down like giant scythes. A rush of wind drags at my hair. I can feel it tugging. As if it wants to suck me up into those slashing sails.

'Where's Noah?' asks Prudence, as we're about to duck through the mill door.

'He must be already inside.'

As soon as we're through the door, the noise hits us. On this floor the sack chain's rattling, sliding through the hole in the trapdoor. But above our heads, there's a terrible racket. Rumbling, clattering, creaking, as if all the machinery is going full speed.

'Upstairs!' yells Mum through the dust and the din.

We go racing upstairs to the stone floor.

'The millstones are turning!' shouts Prudence.

You can hear them thudding around. They're running empty, stone striking off stone.

Through the windows the white sails are flashing by.

'Smoke,' whispers Mum in a horrified voice. 'Look, smoke.'

I can see it now – wisps of grey smoke, coming through the eye of the millstone. It's already making us cough.

'We've got to stop the mill,' shouts Prudence. 'If we don't, it'll go up in flames!'

'Let's find Noah,' says Mum grimly, heading up to the bin floor.

The higher we climb, the more the mill rocks. The great wooden cog wheels are thundering round. You can't hear yourself think. It's like being inside a giant cement mixer. Everything's moving and shaking, even the shadows. The whole mill is shuddering; at any second it'll burst apart like a bomb.

Noah's not on the bin floor. We stagger to the cap floor. Up into wind and brilliant light. The storm hatch is flapping, *bang, bang, bang*. The sails are shrieking past outside – like witches riding through a storm.

'There he is!' yells Prudence, pointing upwards.

Noah's right up in the cap, squashed between moving machinery. Wheels are whirring all round him. The windshaft is turning, levers are clanking. He'll be crushed. What if he slips? One wrong move and he'll be ground up to dog meat.

He's fighting with the brake lever. Leaning all his weight on it, trying to force it down.

'Can you get the brake on?' Mum screams up into the cap.

Noah looks down and sees us. Sweat is dripping off his forehead. He dashes it away with his hand. 'No, it's jammed.'

The brake's sending out sparks like a *Golden Rain* firework.

Ping! An iron bolt blasts like a bullet out of the wall. It nearly got me – just scorched my ear.

'The mill's breaking up!' shouts Mum.

I'm terrified. It feels like we're going to take off. As if the mill's going to rip itself out of the ground and launch into space like a rocket. A picture whizzes through my mind – of our mill, floating in orbit round planet Earth.

Noah comes leaping down out of the cap and crash-lands in a cloud of silvery dust. There's fresh, bright blood on his face where the machinery's clawed him.

He looks up into the wheels. 'She won't let me put on the brake – and anyway, it's too late. She's running too fast. If I put it on now, she won't take the strain. She'll crack into a million pieces.'

'What do we do?' asks Mum.

'You run,' Noah tells us. 'You get out, *fast*.'

He stands firm on the swaying cap floor. 'Clear off!' he says.

He's going to stay until the end. Until the mill breaks up. Like the captain going down with the Titanic –

But my mum thinks she's the captain too. 'It's my windmill,' she tells him. 'I'm staying.'

'No,' I grab her arm. 'Come on.'

Mum and Noah stare at each other with white, scared faces. While around us the machinery's racing on, like runaway horses.

'Let's feed her!' yells Noah suddenly. 'Pour grain in the stones. Try to slow her down. Come on, let's feed her.'

We go staggering down, crashing off walls. The stairs are bucking about, trying to throw us off.

'Stay here,' orders Noah when we get to the stone floor. 'When I send the grain up, tip it into the hopper.'

He goes hurtling downstairs. The smoke's making me choke; the din's battering my ear drums, and I'm seasick, dizzy from the shaking floor.

Bang! The trapdoor flies open. A bag of grain shoots through, hooked to the chain.

We pounce on it, working like demons. We heave the sack up, tip it into the hopper, like feeding a monster through its great wooden gob.

My arms feel like the bones are cracking. The floor's bouncing me about like a trampoline. My eyes are hot and sticky with dust. I'm half-blind. Another bag comes rattling up on the sack chain, we tip that one in. The stones are gobbling grain but still going faster, faster. They're sending blue sparks flying everywhere, making a terrible, teeth-jangling, screechy sound, like chalk on a blackboard, only a zillion times worse.

There's a mighty *crack* somewhere above our heads.

'The upright shaft's going!' screams Mum. 'Get out! Get out!'

More cracking sounds, all over the mill. It's springing apart like a busted clock.

Then the trapdoor flaps go *bang* again and a mushroom head rises through. Noah comes up riding the chain like a circus act. He leaps onto the floor.

He'd scare me to death, if I didn't know he was on our side now. His face is streaky with dust and blood, like grey and red war paint. It's all twisted-up with despair.

'No good,' he gasps. 'She doesn't want feeding. She's fighting us!'

What's he on about? Why does he keep talking as if the mill's a person, as if it's *alive*?

'I think she *wants* to burn down,' Noah tells us. These last words come spitting out of his mouth.

I mean, I'm a staggering, choking, half-blinded wreck – in other words, I'm not feeling too bright. But even I realize, 'That's really stupid.' Mills don't kill themselves, do they? Mills don't commit *suicide*?

But then Mum starts speaking.

'We're not going to hurt you.'

At first I think she's talking to me.

'What?' I yell. 'What?'

Once again, her voice rings out, louder and clearer than before.

'We're not going to hurt you.'

Then I realize she's not talking to me at all. She's gazing upwards. Suddenly, the hairs on the back of my neck start to itch.

'Are you listening?' she shouts, into the rumbling wheels.

I can't believe this is for real. It's too creepy. My mum's *talking* to the mill. Asking it if it's *listening*.

'We're going to look after you, I promise,' Mum's telling the mill. 'We're going to keep you just as you are. We're not going to make you into an office. I'm a Blezzard. I wouldn't do that.'

Did I imagine it? Or are those millstones slowing down?

There's a flash of hope in Noah's face. 'Keep talking,' he says to Mum.

This is crazy. It's madness – like the worst nightmare you ever had. The mill's shaking itself to bits all around us. The stones are running red-hot. But my mum's trying to save it, to *talk* to it, like you'd talk someone down off a ledge.

'Everything will be all right,' she's telling the mill. 'I promise.'

'Stop, please make it stop,' I'm wishing, over

and over, inside my head.

I'm concentrating really hard on wishing, putting my heart and soul into it. And I know Prudence and Noah are wishing too, with all their hearts. Then, suddenly, something makes me put out my right hand and Prudence and Noah are doing it too and we link miller's thumbs and wish, and I can feel the power of the Blezzards surging through us, binding us with an unbreakable bond, making us strong!

'Make it stop.' That's me talking.

'Everything will be all right.' That's Noah.

Then I realize something – the floor's not swaying so much. The crashing and creaking are slowing down. Two cracks, then one, then it stops altogether.

A long time seems to pass before I dare open my eyes.

When I do, I can hardly believe it. The world seems peaceful and calm. As if our ship has sailed safely out of a terrible storm.

'She's slowed down,' says Noah, his face sparkling with happiness. 'She's decided to live! Listen to those millstones.'

They're not scorching round any more. They're turning gently, purring like a cat.

I can see the sails out of the window. They're gliding by, ever so softly, against a blue sky.

It's like magic. The dust's floating back down to the floor. The smoke's clearing. And instead of burning I can smell the lovely, sweet smell of barley meal.

'Phew.' That's me, giving a big, relieved sigh.

It's over. Noah, Prudence and I stare at each

other, in a dazed sort of way. My thumbs are peaceful now. Not even twitching.

Mum looks even more dazed than we do. She's still saying weird things: 'Poor little mill,' she's saying, as if the mill is a scared child. 'It didn't want to be shut down.'

'I told you it listened,' said Noah.

Mum shivers and hugs herself, like she's coming back to her senses. Then she says to Noah, 'You can go up and put the brake on now. And open the slats in the sails.'

Even Prudence looks startled. Because, like me, she expects Noah to scowl and say, 'You do it.' Noah doesn't like people much. He doesn't take orders from anyone.

But Noah just says, 'OK.'

He's half-way up the stairs when Mum says, 'Wait a minute.' Noah turns round. He looks bone-tired. He's swaying, as if he's going to collapse any second.

'I'm going to keep my promise,' says Mum. 'I'm going to keep this mill running. And you can be the miller.'

'You offering me *work*?' asks Noah,

suspiciously, as if he can't believe it.

Mum nods. 'Only a Blezzard could do it.'

And Noah looks really happy – because us Blezzards just saved the mill and because he's got a job.

Then he tramps up into the cap to put on the brake. Mum's checking the damage. Peering into the millstones, tapping at the beams, as if she's been around windmills all her life.

Out of the windows, we can see the sails slowing down, then stopping. Everything's under control.

'That was close.' It's all I can think of to say.

'Wait until Mum and Dad hear about this,' Prudence tells me. She's taking off her coat and her green woolly hat, plus a couple of jumpers. 'I'm hot now,' she says. 'It's all that dragging sacks about.'

She's amazing. You've got to admire her. She sounds really calm and matter-of-fact, as if nothing unusual has happened. As if you stop a mill from committing suicide every day.

'Will your mum and dad believe it?' I ask her. 'About what Noah said, I mean? About the mill being alive and trying to destroy itself because it didn't want to end up as an *office*?'

It can't be true, can it? A windmill can't *think* for itself. It can't work its own machinery. It can't decide, 'I'm *sooo* depressed today, I'm going to burn myself down.'

The brake slipped, that's all. That's what I think. And whatever works the shutters, that went wrong too. It's nothing creepy, nothing weird. There's a simple, logical explanation.

'Come on, your mum and dad won't really believe all that stuff, will they?' I ask Prudence again, almost begging her to say no.

She shrugs. 'What, that Blezzard's Mill has got a mind of its own? Well, they probably *will* believe it. I mean, they're Blezzards aren't they? Nothing about windmills surprises us. We've got –'

'I know, I know,' I groan. 'You don't have to tell me. Us Blezzards have got windmills in our blood.'

CHAPTER 11

Once a Blezzard, always a Blezzard

It's Saturday morning. Me and Prudence are sitting in the paddock at High Cold Knott Farm. We're not doing anything in particular – just watching the lamb that Noah raised skipping about.

'She's our pet lamb now,' says Prudence. 'When she's a big, fat sheep she'll still come running to see us, just like a dog.'

'Will she fetch sticks? Or sit up and beg?'

'You must be joking,' says Prudence. 'Sheep aren't very brainy.'

Talking about being brainy makes me take a quick, sneaky look at Blezzard's Mill. I can't help it. I can't help thinking about that white swivel head, like a skull, with all those whizzing wheels inside.

'Come on!' I tell myself sternly. 'Sheep aren't brainy. And windmills aren't brainy either. Right?'

Anyhow, nothing's whizzing round in the mill now. The machinery's dead. The sails are still – a giant, white cross against the blue sky. The mill looks peaceful and pretty in the sunshine.

But it won't be peaceful for long. Because Mum's keeping her promise. She and Dad worked out this Big Plan. If they have a tea room and open the mill to visitors and sell flour and windmill-shaped souvenirs – then it should make a profit.

Noah's chief windmiller. He's *even* promised to be nice to the visitors. He's probably in there now, getting her ready for the grand opening day.

'Your Noah's working really hard,' I tell

Prudence. 'He's all right, your Noah.'

He's just not very sociable. He prefers windmills to people. There's no law against it.

Prudence frowns, thoughtfully: 'Remember when Noah was up in the cap, trying to put the brake on? I thought the machinery was going to chew him up and spit him out in little chunks. It nearly did, didn't it? He was brave, wasn't he?'

'Yep,' I agree. 'Crazy – but brave. I'm glad he's on our side. After all, us Blezzards should stick together.'

Oh no, did I really say that? I can't believe I said that.

Actually something else happened that I can't believe either. That cool kid is talking to me again. I saw him in the village shop. He came right up to me. 'Hey, Simon,' he said. 'You and me are mates? Right? Give me six!' He was really friendly. I forgot to say, I did have Noah standing next to me at the time.

'There's your mum,' says Prudence, pointing. 'Going to the mill.'

'Yeah, she's got really keen on windmillering. She says she wants to look after it.'

But suddenly, as I'm staring at the mill, it seems to change, right in front of my eyes. I don't see a pretty picture-postcard mill any more – but something much more sinister. I see four slicing arms on a tall black tower with a swivel-head on top. And I'm thinking, 'That mill doesn't need looking after. No way. That mill can take care of itself.'

Then Prudence says something really strange:

'It's a good job your mum's going to look after it. It's supposed to get nasty if people don't look after it.'

'What? What you talking about?'

There's something cold and creepy slithering down my spine.

I recognize it. It's fear. 'What do you mean, it's supposed to get nasty?'

'Oh it's just a story – one of those windmill stories us Blezzards get told when we're little. You sure you don't know it already?'

'No, tell me.'

That fear is spreading out now. Its icy tentacles seem to be hugging my heart.

'I don't suppose it's *true* or anything. It's about Noah Blezzard – the one who's buried in the churchyard. The story says that he wasn't a good miller. That he was drunk all the time and neglected the mill. And once he was so drunk he let the bell ring and ring and didn't answer it and the mill almost burnt down. So it got rid of him.'

'What do you mean, it got rid of him? That's ridiculous.'

I can feel my voice getting high and hysterical, but I can't stop it. 'I thought it was an accident. I thought he fell off the sails!'

Prudence shrugs. 'The story says the mill did it. It waited until he was out on the sails. Then it took off the brakes and made the sails go round faster and faster until he lost his grip and got flung off.'

'Are you saying the mill killed him – because he didn't look after it properly?'

My brain's making great kangaroo leaps, from one wild thought to another.

My mum promised the mill, 'We won't hurt you.' But what if the mill was trying to hurt us? What about Tuesday, when we nearly died in there? What if it wasn't destroying itself but trying to destroy *us*?

I've got to get this straight. 'Are you saying the mill deliberately killed its own miller?' I ask Prudence again.

Prudence looks awkward. 'I wish I'd never told you the story now,' she says.

'Do you believe it?'

I look her straight in the eyes. She tries to slide her eyes away but she can't do it. She's too straightforward and honest for that.

'You *do* believe it, don't you?'

'I don't know,' she says. 'Sometimes, like you, I think it's ridiculous. But sometimes . . .' and here she takes a quick, uneasy glance at the mill, 'sometimes, that mill looks as if it really *could* do something like that.'

'I know what you mean.'

'But anyway,' adds Prudence, 'even if it *was* true, your mum and Noah are looking after the mill, aren't they? They're taking really good care of it. So there's no need to worry.'

I take a good, long squint at Blezzard's Mill. It's changed again, like Jekyll and Hyde. It's beautiful now. The white cap is dazzling, like a glitterball. It doesn't look like it could ever hurt anyone.

Prudence seems to be reading my mind. 'It's a stupid story,' she says. 'It's just an ordinary windmill.'

'Yeah,' I agree with her. 'It's just ordinary.'

Of course it is.

On the other hand –

We go walking down to the mill house, chatting about the Big Plan.

Blezzard's Mill is throwing its dark, crooked shadow across the grass. For a few seconds, while we're walking through that shadow, I can feel myself shivering. I can't help it.

I've already noticed that the storm hatch in the cap is open. And, before I can stop myself, I start shouting up into the sails. 'I'm *really* looking forward to the grand opening day, aren't you, Prudence? I'm really *glad* Blezzard's Mill is going to be working again!'

Prudence glances at me a bit strangely. But then she makes her hands into a megaphone and yells upwards, 'Oh yes, I'm glad too. Ever so glad!'

We look at each other kind of half-embarrassed. But after all, you can't be too careful. The mill might be listening.

I know to ordinary people that sounds crazy. But me and Prudence and Noah, we've got miller's thumbs. We're Blezzards. And nothing *ever* surprises us about windmills.

About the Author

Years ago, I met someone who grew up in a windmill. He told me how he used to ride up and down on the sack hoist chain and how the sails made a swooshing sound, like swans flying over. I thought, 'That's really nice.' But, not long ago, driving through Lincolnshire, I saw a mill, at dusk, on a hill top. The cap was like a head; the sails seemed like giant arms. That mill didn't look nice at all. It looked dark, sinister and threatening. So *Swivel-Head* was born!